HOW TO MAKE PEOPLE LIKE YOU

PROVEN STRATEGIES ON INSTANTLY ATTRACTING OTHERS AND WINNING THEM OVER

STEVEN HOPKINS

CONTENTS

INTRODUCTION

Have you ever wondered why some people are liked and popular while others are not? Well, I want you to know that most of these people know some secret techniques and have successfully applied these techniques to get to their current positions.

What are these secret techniques? As a reader of this book, you will learn what these secrets are and how to apply them.

You might be wondering why you need people to like you. Shouldn't you just 'be yourself and not care what anybody thinks'? Well, think about it this way. We all need people in our lives. Whatever we do in this world, whether directly or indirectly, we want someone to notice and acknowledge it.

Almost everything you can be is dependent on the relationships you build, and when people like you, and you make connections, you will be welcomed with open arms.

Making a new friend, meeting your future in-laws, acing an interview, winning an election, or wooing a partner all depend on people liking you, and this book is structured in a way that makes difficult things easy to understand.

My life has been aimed at helping people. As a life and motivation coach, I specialize in motivation, self-discipline, communication, NLP techniques, psychology, and human behavior. I have been really fortunate to work with so many people either as a personal trainer or coach, helping them discover the secrets of winning, and it all begins with getting people to like you.

I have worked with a lot of people with different backgrounds, beliefs, and professions, and my long years of practice have taught me that everyone has a "soft spot" which they are fond of, and once you can find what that soft spot is, you can access their hearts.

Sometimes I look back and I still can't believe that I once moved my family around the world to start up a digital marketing consultancy business in Singapore. It seems crazy now, but we moved out there knowing just a handful of people, and most of them were business contacts. They were very polite but the relationship wasn't destined to go any further than our business dealings. We had to make friends if we were going to make a real go of living and working there. Michelle is great at making friends and a lot of the advice and suggestions I make in this book come from what I have observed of her. So a lot of the credit must go to her, I suppose!

I have given many seminars, coached, and talked to different groups of people and individuals from different walks of life, and it has been a very exciting and rewarding experience.

To further reach and help more people overcome the different challenges that they face because they can't build proper connections with other people, I have decided to take the advice of friends, colleagues, and people I have worked with and write a book to guide and coach people on the secret of "how to get people to like you."

How to make people like you is an interesting topic I discovered while growing as an entrepreneur. I eventually realized that the art of getting along with people in everyday business is a calculated fine art. The most interesting part is that the topic can be taught and learned.

The human body holds a lot of secrets that, when properly used, can speak volumes and can be used to make total strangers feel comfortable around you while you build rapport.

It is interesting to know that a few gestures and body movements can make people form an impression about you, and when you follow up with a little conversation, you can convert a total stranger into a friend and get them chatting.

Why do you need to read this book? Well, I have a better question in mind. Who doesn't need friends and meaningful connections in life? You will agree with me that in any profession you find yourself, what you need to succeed are people.

While building relationships comes naturally to some people, for some, it is almost an impossible task.

For any of the categories mentioned, the techniques discussed in this book are applicable to all to either improve your existing skills or to learn from scratch how to get people to like you.

Why is it important to be likable?

First, you should understand that being likable is no special inborn gift, but a skill set. And it is learnable.

Here are a few things you need to know about people that are likable:

- People that are likable get elected and promoted more than people that are less likable.
- People that are likable have a more successful life and career. They get easily rewarded and are more popular.
- People that are likable are better salesmen; they close more deals and make more money.
- People that are likable are mostly happier and probably even live longer. Why? Because they get more attention and better service from other people like doctors and other professionals.

According to a Columbia University study by Melinda Tamkins, the success rate between some colleagues in the same workplace is not guaranteed by whom you know but by how popular you are.

The study showed that people that are likable are seen as trustworthy, decisive, and hardworking. They hardly miss out on opportunities as they received recommendations.

The less likable people are more likely seen as arrogant, manipulative, and conniving. They are hardly recommended for any promotions or pay raises, no matter what their education qualifications were.

When you are likable, a lot of things seem to fall into place by themselves. And since likeability is a learnable skill set, you will be on your way to the top after you finish reading this book.

What makes people likable?

After realizing how being likable has a huge impact on your success in life, you wonder, what makes a person likable? Well, simply put, it is their ability to consciously connect with other people and always leave a better impression about themselves.

This book will help you awaken those abilities of

yours that you have failed to put to use. Moreover, this book will help you discover, develop, connect, and put to good use those dormant abilities. In the following chapters, you will learn how to make a good first impression with your body language, how to master small talks, how to develop incredible charisma, and so much more! Now, let's dive right in and start learning about the first, and most important step to make people like you: making a great first impression.

1. MAKING A GREAT FIRST IMPRESSION WITH YOUR BODY LANGUAGE

We don't know where our first impression comes from or precisely what they mean, so we don't always appreciate their fragility.

— MALCOLM GLADWELL

Why First Impressions Are Important for Any Relationship

YOU MIGHT BE WONDERING why you never got a reply to the text you sent to the lady or guy you met at the party last night who you were so sure you had a good conversation with. If this happened to you, or you have been in this kind of situation, then it is time to ask yourself if you created a good first impression.

"Was it the outfit I wore or something I did?" you may ask yourself. As a matter of fact, first impressions matter a lot as they create a lasting image of how someone sees you.

The people we come into contact with every day, ranging from people you say hello to at your office, at the gym, school, to the waiter at your favorite breakfast spot, could be a potential friend, someone you might need help from, or even a lover/spouse. You make contact with these people not even realizing what a brief interaction can bring about tomorrow.

Every contact comes with a great opportunity for what may be tomorrow, but the key to deciding on whether the meeting will materialize or turn into something bigger is the first impression you make.

Let me illustrate this with an example from my own life. As a young entrepreneur trying to get projects off the ground I wanted to put myself in a position where I was earning more money for my young family, especially with our firstborn, Sammy, on the way. I had some ideas for health drinks and gym equipment and needed to get private investors on board. One of the guys I went to meet at his office, didn't end up investing in the idea I had first presented to him, but we ended up in the elevator afterwards and chatted about children. He was only too happy to impart some advice and although the business meeting had officially ended in his office, this ending in the car park was very positive and we both remembered it. The next time I went to him with an idea in need of funding, he already had a positive first impression associated with me.

Now you should start believing the saying that a first impression is always important, and we don't get to make another.

The Power of Nonverbal Communication

Since more than half of communication is through body language, this is a very important subject. At the end of this section, you will understand the power of nonverbal communication and why it is so powerful.

Nonverbal communication is usually the way you look, listen, react, or the signs you give a person to show if you are following the conversation, agree or disagree with a proposition, and whether you care or not.

In a situation where you are conversing with someone and what you are saying matches with the nonverbal communication you make, it builds trust and a relationship. And if it doesn't, there might be confusion or tension.

For instance, when you are sitting in a cafeteria and someone walks up to you to ask if the seat next to you is taken, if your answer is "No" with your head nodding, you might sound dishonest. And, with nonverbal communication being a natural language that transmits your actual feelings, the person will likely go with your nonverbal connotation.

In order to show your true intentions, make sure your nonverbal language is well utilized during a conversation. When it is well utilized, you look more honest, confident, lively, and likable.

So instead of just saying "No," you can add more

body language by smiling and using other parts of your body.

Smile

I know you feel this sounds so simple and might be wondering what a smile has to do with people liking you. Here is a fact you have to know: smiling is a powerful way to easily make people like you.

Maybe you would think that smiling all the time is simply inauthentic, but think about this: when you smile, you immediately create a bond or connection between you and the other person, making the person glad to talk to you. It does the magic by sparking some kind of a pleasing response from the person involved, and this can also come in the form of a responsive smile.

Smiling is a trick I always use that has worked countless times. Since I know people generally believe smiling is contagious and would rather be around someone with a cheerful and beautiful smile than the person giving a stern look, why not just use the trick in your favor?

This is very important because you feel connected

to a smile emotionally and physically. Also, the brain releases endorphins whenever you smile. This triggers a feeling of peace and happiness. Many times, people link this feeling with the personality responsible for it.

So, if you don't have a smile on your face or lack the skills for one, it's time to devote some quality time to your mirror by standing in front of it and learning how to smile. If you are around people, whenever possible, try as much as possible to smile, and you will soon find out how simple yet effective it is just to put on a beautiful smile on your face.

Make Gentle Eye Contact

To create a first impression when you want to make people like you, making eye contact plays a major role, and it is a big step to take. With the use of gentle eye contact, you project great confidence that is generally perceived as attractive.

On the other hand, people who are not able to look others straight in their eyes are seen as dishonest, untrustworthy, and lacking in confidence. Just imagine: if you are talking to someone and you hardly see this person's eyes, wouldn't you find this person untrustworthy and simply don't want to talk with him or her anymore? If you agree with me, pay attention to your own eye contact when you are talking with someone!

I believe that eye contact brings about trust and indicates honesty and sincerity—and we all know that getting someone to like you involves making that person trust you. Therefore, keep that in mind when you are trying to connect with anyone.

To practice eye contact, find a person you can trust and let him or her know that you are trying to improve your communication skills, then, try the following strategies:

1. Establish eye contact right away: establish eye contact even before you start talking.
2. Use the 50/70 rule: to avoid staring and making the person feel uncomfortable, maintain eye contact for 50% of the time while speaking, and 70% of the time while listening.
3. Look from side-to-side: if maintaining eye contact is too difficult to you, try to look into that person's eyes and hold it for 4-5

seconds, and then slowly glance to
the side.

4. If you can't maintain eye contact, you can
    also look at an eyebrow or the space
    between the eyes and mouth.

5. Avoid looking down: doing this can give
    an impression that you lack confidence.
    Tell the other person to let you know if he
    or she sees you do this.

6. Practice: it is natural for some people to
    establish eye contact. However, it's okay
    if it doesn't come naturally to you. Keep
    practicing, and remember to remind
    yourself to maintain gentle eye contact
    whenever you are talking to other
    people.

Mirror their body language

Getting people to like you can be somewhat tricky,
but if done with the methods I have put together, it
becomes easier. It has worked for me, my clients,
and a whole lot of other people.

When making a first and lasting impression, you
can employ the use of mirroring the other person's

position. It is a proven fact that people tend to like those that are similar to themselves.

Take your time to observe someone. If you realize the person you meet is quiet and calm, you should also find a way to act that way. If the person likes smiling, give him or her lots of smiles too. And if you meet a person that talks a lot, try to keep up! Trust me, I have used this technique to make a lot of friends.

Always check the person's posture and gestures to know how to act. Is the person feeling relaxed or uptight? Is he or she looking nervous, tense, or anxious? Study them carefully to match the position. This will make them like you subconsciously because they feel that you understand them or are similar to them.

Make Physical Contact

Over the years, the psychology of physical contact has been a fascination for researchers and people in general. People are curious to know why physical contact can be so influential.

You might be asking yourself questions like "How

does simple physical contact make you do something you never thought you would?"

To be honest, it has also been a fascination for me and I believe it must have crossed your mind too. The truth is: when physical contact is made, oxytocin, serotonin, and dopamine, which are also called the "happy chemicals," are released inside the human brain.

The reaction triggered by the "happy chemicals" lowers the level of cortisol, which is the stress hormone. The lowered cortisol levels make you feel relaxed, slow down your heart rate, and reduce your stress level. Invariably, physical contact can trigger comfort.

With a lot of studies backing up claims that a simple touch can greatly affect and boost your chances of having your way with people, it is a strategy to put into practice.

Most communication is made through physical contact. Just think about it: physical contact is involved when you offer someone a handshake, when you pat someone on the back, or give someone a bear hug.

When you touch someone, they don't notice it easily, but a reaction is taking place inside their body. A simple touch can put the person in the mood and can immediately spark a relationship since he or she will be feeling relaxed and interested in hearing what you think.

At the end of it all, you have to coordinate your body language to gain that good first impression and trust. So smile, make gentle eye contact, mirror their positioning, and touch them if you need to.

When getting someone to like you, your aim at creating a relationship is to share a common ground. I believe this chapter has been able to clear up some misconceptions about a first impression and has pointed out why it is very important to make a good one. In my book, *How to Talk to Anyone*, I talk more in depth about first impressions and how important they are when you want to build a long-lasting relationship with someone.

The next chapter involves verbal communication. There, you will be learning how to use powerful small-talk techniques to make people like you, almost instantly.

What We've Learned

- First impressions are crucial for any relationship. If you can make a good first impression, everything else will become easier
- Employ the power of nonverbal communication (smile, eye contact, physical touch etc.) to enhance your relationship

2. POWERFUL SMALL-TALK TECHNIQUES

> *Communication - the human connection - is the key to personal and career success.*
>
> — PAUL J. MEYER

SOMETIMES, small talk can feel meaningless, especially if you don't go beyond the current weather or what you might've eaten for lunch that day. However, you have to remember that small talks are just the first step towards getting to bigger conversations. Here are a few useful techniques to master the art of small talk:

Ask people about themselves

It is good that you have created a first impression with someone you just met, and you were able to use the right body language and coordination. You smiled and made gentle eye contact, fair enough; you followed through with mirroring some of their traits like positioning, and it worked. Good for you. Now that you have succeeded in attracting their attention, what next?

It's time to follow up with conversation. To create bonds and build trust, having a good conversation is key.

Who Can Engage in Small Talk?

If your personality is that of an introvert, there is a big possibility that you are not a big fan of small talk, and people might get the wrong idea about you, thinking you don't like other people. But as we both know, this is simply not true. You just have to conquer your limiting beliefs and practice.

Remember, conversation is a two-way thing and you need to do the talking and the listening at the same time. Anybody can become an expert at conversation; you can master small talk once you understand the techniques to apply.

As you read on, you will find handy techniques that can help you sail through that awkward silence, especially in a situation where you suddenly become tongue-tied instead of building the intended rapport.

Let me tell you a story. I remember one time during my college years, I was riding a bus, and sitting next to me was this beautiful lady who looked like a really interesting person. She had a lovely smile on her face.

I wanted to start a conversation with her, but then I was suddenly overwhelmed with this feeling of self-consciousness. So many thoughts started running through my mind: "Am I good enough to talk to her? Will she find me interesting? Will she ignore me? Where do I even start?"

These types of questions can make you feel tongue-tied and lose the rapport you want to create. Eventually, I didn't even get a chance to talk to this lady, and that was all because of my fear of small talk. After that, I made a decision to over-come my inner fear, and built strong self-confidence to be able to talk to anyone.

So where do you start? Well, if I can give you one piece of advice, I would say that the secret to keep a conversation going is to get the other person talking.

Ask More Questions

A good way to get the conversation rolling is by asking people questions about themselves. This is really effective, especially when you really don't know what to say. Get the person talking and make them share the things they like most, what matters to them, and things they consider as their favorites.

A proper conversation is a two-way street. Asking about the other person is a way of showing interest and a good way to learn and even hear a story about their experiences or their past. Questions are rather non-judgmental inquiries, and most people let their guard down when they sense care or concern from your questions. Besides, people generally like it when they are the center of attention. Hence, you make the other party feel good about themselves.

In the realm of small talk, the most important thing to remember is when to stop talking and start asking. From the responses of your partner, you pick clues and hints to be able to decide when it's time to stop talking.

Try to ask the other person's opinion about things and compliment them when necessary. Let's take the example of my business meeting for funding that ended up with me chatting with the guy about babies in the car park. That came from his willingness to share advice and my willingness to sit back and let him talk. I asked him questions here and there but nothing too probing. Instead I let him reveal himself.

When asking questions, remember that there are two ways to ask questions – the open questions that demand a long answer and the closed questions that mostly require a "yes" or "no" answer.

It's better to go with the open questions that will get the other party talking for a while, so you can listen more and show that you are interested in them. The spotlight will be on the other party and you can probe more. Be conscious of closed questions as the short answers might leave you struggling for the next thing to say.

Talk About what interests the other person

When you talk about what interests the other party, you will probably get them going on and on, taking the pressure off you and giving you enough room for the next question. To begin the conversation, find common ground, a general topic that can connect both of you and which you can both converse about.

The occasion for the meeting will determine the tone of the conversation. For example, "The hall looks well lit, don't you agree?" "Beautiful weather tonight, isn't it?" "The program was really awesome. How did you feel about it?" "My wife is a great fan of your work. How long have you been writing?" All these questions are preparing the conversational ground.

Good follow-up questions can be "Who do you think plays better?" "Where can I get something like this?" "What do you think about the performance tonight?" Hearing your question, the other party will be inclined to give you a long explanation because your question is an open question and it concerns what interests them.

Lead the conversation

When the other party feels they are in charge, make them believe they are truly in control; that way you can steer the conversation in any direction you want.

However, the key to keeping open questions flowing is using the 'Who, Where, What, Why, When, and How' method to maintain the tempo and length of the conversation.

When you apply the open method of questioning, you will surely find out what they are interested in. Questions like, "Where do you think that came from?" "How do you want this to be?" "Which one would you recommend and why, please?" Yes! These questions will surely leave the other person with no choice but to offer an explanation, description, or to tell a short story.

Use their Name or Nickname

People love hearing their names. At every good opportunity, try to call them by their first name or nickname and you will be creating the opportunity for them to like you since you are feeding their pleasure centers.

When people hear their name, it will further draw them in and reward the pleasure centers of their brain. People love it when they hear the sound of their own name; it can make the rapport you are building take sudden shape. When you call out their name, you are telling them how important they are, and they will most certainly be interested in you. They will remember how you make them feel, which in turn makes them feel happier and reassured.

By subconsciously planting positive feelings in someone when you mention their name, they will form an impression of you and feel you are connected to them in a positive way, and that will amp up your likeability level.

Bring Along Your Sense of Humor

People pay money for others to make them laugh; you can see that happening at stand-up comedy shows and when clowns are invited to events.

A sense of humor can actually improve your likeability. It is human nature, and also logical that humans would rather be around those who make them feel happy and good. A good sense of humor can help you get on the good side of many people.

It's Hard to Hate a Jokester

Cracking a joke or two is a smart way to break the silence, get people to relax around you, or create a lasting impression around new people. For example, maybe you mentioned your name earlier to someone, but this person just didn't remember your name.

The other person might politely ask, "Sorry, I'm quite terrible with names; what was your name again?" Maybe your name is Paul Coleman. You could create a little humor by saying, "I'm Paul Coleman, but my friends call me PC." You could add, "When you hear them call me PC, you might even think I build them, or I'm a walking personal computer. Don't be deceived though."

Seeing you as someone who has a carefree approach to life will get most people to smile and call you that name your friends call you. They are telling you they also want to be friends by calling you "PC" instead of "Paul Coleman."

Most People Like a Room Filled with Laughter

The most liked people are those who can keep the room lively and filled with laughter. Regardless of how people picture their ideal friend or romantic partner, they will always be comfortable around someone with a sense of humor.

A study from researchers at DePaul University and Illinois State University found that when you are first getting to know someone, using humor can make the other person like you more. The study further suggested that participating in humorous tasks together can further increase romantic attraction, quicken the bond of friendship, or get people to easily like you.

Laugh easily and smile often

When you smile a lot and laugh openly, you can easily win people over. Giving a big and natural smile when you meet someone for the first time will mostly guarantee that they will remember you later.

I had two home teachers when I was a kid; one often smiled when he taught and would politely call my name before he explained whatever I didn't understand. It was easy for me to understand whatever he taught me and I always looked forward to his lessons.

The other teacher was not as friendly as the first. He never smiled, and it felt like he hated me, or he at least hated teaching me. Well, as a kid I naturally developed a resistance to him and I preferred to spend more time with the teacher who smiled. I would rather ask him about things I didn't understand than ask the other home teacher.

Make People Feel Good

Since people are different, how can you know how to make them feel good about themselves? Well, it is quite universal because people prefer to be perceived the way they see themselves. Everyone has their own beliefs about themselves and their perceived selves are aligned to that.

The universal characteristics of everyone include wanting happiness, more attention, love and care, and being useful and productive. When people get those vibes, they will surely like you.

This experience is described by the self-verification theory. Everyone wants confirmation of our views, positive or negative.

They Feel Good; You Feel Good

When you talk about people and they feel good about themselves, they will feel good about you. However, watch what you say. You don't have to be unduly positive, or else they might feel you are either naïve or just overly flattering them. Intelligently comment on the good you see and avoid talking bad about things or people.

When you complain about others, the impression you give your listener is that they may be your next victim to lose your respect and end up being in your negative book. It goes further as they might also link your complaints with your character and view your complaints as your true self.

Tip: Never ever badmouth your former employer, no matter what previously happened. This is something you should take note of, especially during a job interview.

Compliment Them

Everyone has an image of who they feel they are and sharing compliments with them can really make them feel good about themselves. If you do so, the bond between you and the people you meet will increase. Sounds simple right? Sure, it is. People love a well-timed, genuine compliment, but there are ways to go about how you dish out those compliments in order to leave your conversation on a more positive note.

The key to perfect compliments is not to be false, but genuine, a little bit unique, and well timed.

Be Specific

When you give compliments, don't just tell the person, "You are gorgeous." Tell them why you think they are gorgeous. "The dress is a perfect match for you and you really look gorgeous in it." This type of compliment is specific and based on experience and fact, and people will be inclined to like you more.

Praise Their Efforts

People love validation, whatever field it may be in. After exhausting lots of efforts, nothing beats being acknowledged and getting a compliment.

Don't just say, "Nice speech." Tell the person why you think the speech was nice, because he or she may have exhausted a ton of effort to put the talk together. "You delivered a nice speech. I really love that point (fill in the blank) that you talked about."

When you give compliments, always give the

reason why you feel that way or why a person deserves the compliment.

What We've Learned

- Getting people to talk about themselves is a terrific way to keep the conversation going.
- Calling people by their name creates a sense of importance.
- Everyone is naturally drawn to a calm and relaxed environment. Make people comfortable by complimenting them.

3. START WITH YOURSELF

> *Friendship with oneself is all-important because without it, one cannot be friends with anyone else in the world.*
>
> *Eleanor Roosevelt*

Like Yourself

BEFORE GETTING people to like you, like yourself first! For people to like you, you need to get busy liking yourself. However you treat yourself is how other people will see you. So basically, you attract what you are.

Once you love yourself, you will attract the same

force, attracting more love into your life, and getting more people to trust you.

With the years of experience I have gathered in psychology, I've come to realize that it is difficult to get anyone to like you if you don't possess the characteristics of self-love. How can someone like you when you don't feel happy about yourself? Well, I don't blame them if they don't; no one wants to associate with a sad fellow.

Self-love gives you inner peace, fulfillment, and contentment. If you have self-love, you are happy with yourself and your life generally.

Have you heard a story of someone who claimed to be rich, but who ended up committing suicide? It's sad and is something that always shocks me. There isn't a single one of us who is immune to the impact of low self-esteem.

I went through a lot of failure before finding the keys to success that I am sharing with you now. Working my dull office job, before I became a personal trainer, was something that brought me down every single day. Similarly, suffering failures years later, with the gym-related business products

I tried to market, I was brought low. I had a baby on the way and needed to make more money. There are few things more heartbreaking than knowing you cannot provide enough for your family. When you begin to feel down, you start to see all your failings and it snowballs into a bigger malaise.

I have come to realize that most of the people that fall under this category are people that don't have enough self-love. They see their life as an act, harboring negative thoughts that overpower their clear judgment.

Have you ever been around people and felt you need to talk less to be noticed due to feeling intimidated? Or have you looked at yourself in the mirror and felt you are looking too fat or too slim? You are not alone; I have been down that road too.

Seeing too many flaws in how you naturally look will lower your self-confidence and your thoughts might become negative. You are not better off doing that; rather, take action and love yourself more.

Never allow those thoughts to influence how you react. You should act on thoughts that will bring out your true self. Change what you can about yourself and let that confidence show. Apply a zero-tolerance to any form of self-critique.

Also, forcing yourself to be someone you are not won't do you any good; rather, focus on yourself and make yourself happy. Once you start forcing things, people around you will notice, and it will be too obvious you are acting as something you are not.

Practice Personal Hygiene

The topic "personal hygiene" is an important one to discuss in this book as it can help some people that face challenges making friends due to negligence. I will have to be candid as I proceed—you will have to pardon me! But trust me, it will do you a whole lot of good.

So, our parents were right, after all. Practicing good personal hygiene not only promotes good health but has other benefits in life. Bad personal hygiene can repel people—and I don't blame them after all.

Just put yourself in their shoes. If someone you know hasn't had their bath or smells, I am sure you will try as much as possible to avoid that person, right? So you understand how important it is to keep yourself nice and clean.

We all need to wash our hands, bathe regularly, and brush and floss our teeth to help keep viruses, bacteria, and illnesses away from our body. This entails keeping good personal hygiene, and not only does it have its physical benefits, it also has its mental benefits.

With proper personal hygiene, not only will people see you as clean and tidy, but you will also feel good about yourself. A person with bad personal hygiene normally has a bad odor coming from his or her body or mouth, disheveled hair, and tattered clothes—and oftentimes faces discrimination from people.

On the good side, some people practice great personal hygiene in their daily life. Effortlessly, they brush their teeth, have their bath, see their dentist for routine checkups, and always wash their hands before eating. So, you see, if they can do it, so can you.

You can start by bathing and washing your hair

regularly. Our body constantly sheds skin as some of the skin needs to come off to avoid caking and causing illness. Shave off some of that hair if you need to; clean and cut your nails when they are long; brush and floss your teeth, and at regular intervals, use mint gums or a breath mint.

Normally, you are supposed to brush your teeth immediately after every meal to reduce the accumulation of bacteria in your mouth. This bacterium can cause mouth odor, tooth decay, and gum disease. However, you should be able to brush at least twice daily.

Making it part of you might not be easy at first, but with dedication and persistence, it will become part of you. Also, you can start using a deodorant if you don't have one, and change your clothes every day.

Once your inner and physical body is well taken care of, the next thing to look forward to is the way to dress. Before stepping out, always look in the mirror to check if you look good and feel confident about yourself.

Dress to Impress

This might sound so cliché, but it is definitely something that comes in handy to know. The way you are dressed is the way you will be addressed. My teacher might have said that line again and again, but I only understood the true meaning of it when I started meeting people in places I wasn't familiar with.

If you have ever raised an eyebrow when you see someone wearing tattered clothes or mixing different colors that are too bright, you are not the only one. I am also guilty of this. On a more serious note, you will appreciate a well-dressed man more than a man that is scruffily dressed.

Dressing boosts your confidence

I remember that feeling I have when I know I have outdone myself and dressed better than other days. I smiled more, talked to people more, and was more than willing to make new friends. That was my confidence talking.

Dressing well will boost your confidence, not just

from putting the right outfit together but from the compliments you will receive from people and the way they will stare at you. So, have you realized why you need to dress well?

Dressing creates a first impression

First impressions do matter a lot. By now you should know why it is important to create a good first impression for people to like you.

You shouldn't just dress how you feel, but you should dress the way you want people to see you. If you portray yourself as an unserious person with your dressing, people will take you that way, and if you are looking serious, people will also take you seriously. That's how our dressing addresses us.

Dressing reflects your personality

Of course, our dressing reflects our personality. A banker can't be dressed as a factory worker, nor can a doctor dress as an athlete.

I was guilty of not paying attention to the way I dressed until I realized we are judged on our clothes. Before I could be taken seriously, I had to dress to look serious. At first, I was reluctant to always take note of my dressing before I went out to seminars and lectures, but I later found out my dressing also speaks to the audience.

Opinions are formed in minutes, or even seconds! There are times when people, without even knowing who you are or anything about you, jump to conclusions. Yes, I know it is not ideal to judge people without giving them a chance, but think of it, the human brain is wired to pick clues and inference from what it can see.

Hence, if you already gave a horrible impression through your clothing, you might not even be given the chance to correct it. Are you going to rush to change your clothing?

I guess not!

Hence, your dressing speaks highly of who you are, reflecting the kind of personality you are. This in turn makes people decide if you are worth a friend or not.

Wear Clothes That Fit

You shouldn't just wear clothes but endeavor to wear ones that fit. Some people get comfortable wearing clothes that are bigger than them. It might be a convenient thing to do, but it doesn't present you in the best way.

Wearing a size ten when you are a size nine will not look good on you. It will look loose and shabby, and it won't fit you. On the other hand, clothes that are too small will only end up showing most of your body parts, and it doesn't look professional or comfortable either.

Go for clothes that are well tailored to your body type, and people will start thinking that you are a person with good taste and end up liking you.

Buy quality instead of quantity

A lot of people are of the opinion that having plenty of stuff reflects comfort. Well, I beg to differ; that is not the case. When we have few but quality things, it makes our life more organized and simpler.

It's better to opt for quality clothes instead of buying heaps of clothes that will soon get worn out and which you will end up disposing of. You should invest in quality clothes that reflect your style and personality instead of buying loads of clothes all in the name of having many.

A less complicated lifestyle will do you a lot of good. Embrace the mindset of a simple life, seeing fewer things as more.

Dressing to impress doesn't mean that you have to wear one style of clothing all the time, but rather, wear something that fits, makes you stay confident, reflects your personality, and creates a good first impression on the people you meet.

Spend time with people who improve your image

It is a sad truth, but as humans, we all tend to be judgmental; we easily evaluate someone we meet in just seconds. The same thing applies to you. Bear in mind that people you meet evaluate you immediately. They may be right or wrong with their results, but it's just how the human mind is wired.

Just imagine a mathematics equation that looks difficult at first glance. Most of us won't attempt it because we have the notion that it is difficult to solve. The same concept applies to people. We write off what we don't like. If you've ever found yourself in a situation where you are being criticized, you might be indirectly/unknowingly responsible for the criticism.

You are judged by your company

The ancient proverb, "birds of a feather flock together" provides a terrific explanation of the fact that people with common attributes move together. In other words, people that share similarities are inclined to always spend time with each other.

We get judged by the kind of company we keep. If you hang out with a group of geeks, there is a high chance that you will also be seen as one even if you are not. Also, if your choice of friends always look tattered, it will be difficult for people to separate you from them even if you are the neat one.

To sum up, your choice of friends should always portray the image of how you want people to see you. Otherwise, you might be misjudged by other people.

What We've Learned

- Liking yourself is the very first step to get others to like you
- Take time to look after yourself. You can do this by practicing personal hygiene and wear clothes that fit you and of high-quality.
- Concentrate on being around people that challenge and improve you

4. THREE WAYS TO DEVELOP INCREDIBLE CHARISMA

 *Charisma is the fragrance of the soul.*

Toba Beta

THERE ARE some people who just seem to have that "thing". When they show up in a room, when they are talking, when they are speaking in front of people...they seem to have "something" that just make people like, respect and listen to them. What is that?

Well, it's something called "charisma", and that's exactly what you will learn to develop in this chapter.

Generally, people perceived as being charismatic

possess some unique characteristics that are dynamic, powerful, and charming.

People with charisma have the power to draw other people close to them and to sell their ideas effortlessly. They have the aura to be in charge and command a room.

Charisma is not inborn but something that is learned. No matter the level of success one attains in life, charisma has played an important role in attaining that feat.

Often, it is believed that people that are easily likable are born that way. But have you thought for a second that each and every one of us can actually possess charisma? Here is the thing—there are some methods that can be applied to your lifestyle to make people perceive you as influential, responsible, honest, and trustworthy.

In this chapter, we will be discussing the three ways to develop incredible charisma.

1. Be Present During Conversations

Seeing charisma as the power to outshine others or look better than they are is far from the true meaning. Being charismatic is not about boasting about your good qualities but rather about making other people feel good and well listened to.

The true way to display charisma is to always make other people feel important, and when they have a conversation with you, they will feel better knowing they have your attention.

When you are in an important conversation with someone and you notice he or she is looking distracted and you hardly have his attention, I can imagine how angry and upset you feel about that. You are not alone in this. I have also been in such situations, and I am sure that I have been like this to others before.

I discovered through my discussions with my life coach and mentor, Linda Vale, that I had held on to the sadness of my parent's divorce since it happened when I was six. Linda helped me to realize that it was this fear of being abandoned that led me to push people away from the outset, and this extended to all my conversations and interactions with others. Luckily, she helped me realize what I needed to work on, and now I listen to others with all my attention.

Have you experienced this before? When you are talking to someone, he or she just seems to be distracted and is not really listening.

If you feel bad when in that kind of situation, also imagine putting someone in the same situation. If I am not mistaken, you won't run to the person who doesn't seem to be present during a conversation to pour out your heart next time. It suggests you no longer trust the person.

No matter how insignificant the conversation is, always put your full concentration into it by being present.

Focus your energy on the person to create a feeling of importance

If you want to get the person engaged and create a feeling of importance, then your mental and emotional energy will be put to use—focus it on them. As we discussed earlier, people have an affinity for being recognized and known.

For this to take place, you don't have to go out of your way. Create situations to make the person feel happy and confident. When they feel all this, it makes them feel important and eager to engage more with you.

Practice effective eye contact

I have come to realize that people who make use of eye contact in sending a message are seen as being honest, confident, truthfully, charming, and hard-working. These results aren't just the reaction you get; the quality of your conversation is also improved.

There is power in the eyes as they convey a message that will allow the receiver to feel heard, more connected, and positive about the message.

To practice eye contact, pay attention to whether you can hold gaze with someone during a conversation. When talking, tilt your head forward and look the person in the eyes. This will make the other person feel important and he or she will be inclined to trust you more.

People like attention... so give it

No one will be comfortable talking with you when you are looking out the window or hardly concentrating.

Presence lies in the mind. You cannot give full attention to a conversation when your mind is somewhere else. To give your full attention, concentrate on the sensations you feel and use them as a point of contact.

The sensations can be your hands touching the table you are seated at or the shoes you are wearing. Just take a moment to concentrate on them to let them constantly remind you that you need to be present.

Keep your devices out of sight

I don't know about you, but I definitely don't like talking to someone that has headphones on or whose phone rings every second.

Putting your devices on vibrate doesn't solve the situation; you should keep them away to reduce the urge for you to check them at any given opportunity. That also tells the other party that you are giving him or her your full attention.

Try it! Next time you are talking to a person, turn your phone to vibrate and put your cellphone in your bag. You will be amazed how this simple act changes the whole conversation.

Be expressive with your body

Using eye contact is not the only way to show your presence. You can use body language. There are gestures you can use to show this—nodding your head and doing thumbs-up to show agreement.

However, be careful to not overdo this, since overdoing this can reduce the person's perception of you. Only use your body language at the appropriate time for you to be taken seriously.

2. Develop a Sense of Confidence

You can easily build and maintain your confidence by regularly working out, feeling and looking good with your dress sense, and indulging in talking about things that you understand.

Individuals with charming personalities are usually very powerful. Although it doesn't mean that they have to be the leaders of the free world or the heads of a large organization,

Being powerful means you have the ability to bring about a positive change to your immediate society either through your physical capability, intelligence, know-how, wealth, or fame.

Become physically fit

People will notice the shape of your body the very first time they meet you. Looking all muscular and fit will quickly pass a message across to the most primitive parts of the other's mind about your potency and strength.

Your physical build or fitness also sends messages to people that you can withstand undue fatigue in the course of trying to achieve a certain aim and objective. No wonder we see men with an average-to-husky build tend to earn more than their out of shape and thin contemporaries.

With evidence to back this assertion, the *Wall Street Journal* reported on a study that found average-weight men earn more than their skinny peers. Therefore, if you want to be more self-confident, make sure you spend some time taking care of your body shape.

Have a purpose to live for

Confident and charismatic people always have a purpose in life. They have leverage and the ability to make a positive impact on their immediate society. There is a general impression that powerful people can easily get things done.

With the proper charisma, people will be easily attracted to you like a magnetic force or gravitational attraction. The root behind a magnetic force of attraction is power. Comparing it to the era of ancient cavemen, survival then depended greatly on congenial interaction with those at the top of the social hierarchy because they were the ones that could offer protection, food, and a mate.

For better survival, we need to set a goal, initiate an innovation, have a vision, and follow it with full dedication. People always want to have something to have faith in. If you want to make your dreams reality, then you need to strongly believe and hold onto them. Always have confidence in yourself in any situation.

Create the impression you know your endpoint even if you are not completely sure of the outcome. Leave people with the benefit of the doubt.

Feel confident and powerful

The act of being powerful has to do with your mindset. In fact, that is the starting point. You will carry others along if you show bravery and strength. As the saying goes *"fortune smiles on the brave,"* you have to be brave and confident to become fortunate.

When you are self-assured, you will always draw people close to you in the quest of trying to know you well.

The act of developing confidence is a gradual process that deserves to be given its own accolade. You should also know that the end goal of developing confidence is mastery. When you master anything, the way you think and go about things completely changes.

Whenever you are not sure of the destination, take advantage of whatever comes your way. Even in the moments when we do things we wouldn't normally do, we should always continue to thrive and excel.

3. Know how to talk effectively

If you find it difficult to start and maintain a conversation, you will need creativity. Think about it: what are the things you like from a person you so much admire? What will he or she like to talk about?

A charismatic person has a way with words and knows how to talk to people. Starting a conversation, leading the conversation down the right path, and getting people involved is effortless for them. If you don't know how to do this, then you need to start practicing.

Here are a few tips that you can use to improve your conversation skills:

1. Organize your thoughts: think before you say anything. If you can organize your thoughts, what you say will make more sense to your audience.

2. Be concise: don't use a lot of words to describe something simple. Ask your friends and family to give you some advice on this.

3. Be real: each of us is unique. When you are speaking, you should be natural and let the real you come through.

At first, it will be difficult, but once you are determined, and with lots of practice, you will get better at it. There are many groups, such as ToastMasters that are dedicated to improving your speaking skills. If you don't know where to start, look for a supportive group near your area and start from there.

Use humor as a tool

A person that knows how to sustain a conversation also knows how to make people laugh. Once you can make them happy, they will like you.

Share stories and experiences by using humor. If your story is not that funny, tell it in a way to make it sound funny. Before you tell a joke, think it through because it will be embarrassing to tell a joke and have it fall flat.

However, if that does happen, don't let that discourage you. Just remember that practice makes perfect. If no one laughs when you tell a joke, change the way you tell it and try again next time. Eventually you will find your own speaking style and develop strong charisma.

Ask questions

Asking questions doesn't show that you are dumb. Rather, if you ask questions, it gives you control. To show charisma, ask smart questions.

People that are curious to know more, and who ask questions, are usually portrayed as being intelligent. It is interesting to know that people who ask many questions give the best impression.

Think about our teachers in the classroom. They always tend to ask questions even when they know the answer. We see them as all-knowing and devoid of any fault. Being charismatic is getting to know others more than yourself.

The interviewers we see on TV ask a whole lot of questions of their guests but are hardly irritable since they are good with humor—and viewers love them for that. They seem in control and come across as charismatic individuals as they do their job.

You can only know how someone feels if you go close to them. Ask them questions to understand, know where they are coming from, and how they feel.

In conclusion, having charisma is not innate—you are not born with it. It is something you learn. With the three methods I have provided – be present, be confident and develop your communication skills, I believe that you will become a charismatic person in no time.

After reading the above techniques, make sure you put them to practice until they become a part of you. Once you master charisma, you will be able to wield power and have positive effects on people.

What We've Learned

- Being charismatic naturally draws others to you
- Be present and attentive in conversation —that includes your body, soul, and spirit
- Be confident and have something you believe in as your driving force
- Know how to make people feel comfortable around you

5. HOW TO ATTRACT AND MAKE GREAT FRIENDS

66 *Some people go to priests, others to poetry, I to my friends.*

Virginia Woolf

Be yourself; everyone is unique

BEING unique is a great way to get people to like you, and in order to be unique, you need to be yourself. There are no two people on earth who are exactly the same; we are all unique in our own different ways.

Everyone has different behaviors, personalities, beliefs, and ways of doing things. When in the midst of friends, show them what you've got! You don't need to pretend to be another person just to fit in; rather, show your unique skills and you will be surprised at the way you gain acceptance. One thing I know for sure is that people that exude confidence are easily liked.

In our world today, it is always a challenge to be yourself, especially when we see conformity as a norm. Well, the good news is that you don't have to try to join the majority; you can choose to be yourself and still attract great friends.

It is when you are unique that you attract terrific people who are genuinely attracted to the real you —the potential in you. And the fact is that you are more likely to attract and retain friends when you are yourself rather than when you're trying to be another person. This is because people see you as who you are; there is no need to wear various masks just to fit in and please people.

Set your standards and don't over-please people

It is not a bad idea or a wrong thing to try to please people, but it shouldn't turn out to affect you negatively. When you want to do something that will please a friend, acquaintance, family, or your boss, you are not in any way doing the wrong thing at all. However, note that in the course of trying to please the people around you, you might also, in turn, be going out of your way.

People with standards are seen as highly principled and well respected by their peers. Don't get me wrong: it is never a bad idea to please people—just don't overdo it. The people you are trying to please might start finding it irritating and less attractive when you are not confident of your standard.

When you have standard, there is a huge chance you will attract people who find you charming; people who are wowed by your standard. And best of it all, this might be the criteria for retaining great friends. Don't forget the saying, "birds of a feather, flock together." Hence, with your standard, you will likely attract and retain friends who are fascinated by it.

If you find yourself in a situation where you are feeling shy or not capable of saying no to a friend or a family member who always ask for money from you, then you should know you will be giving that person more opportunity to demand more from you. Always let them know how you feel and where you stand on things.

There is no way you are going to be mentally alert when all you do is try to please everyone close to you with your precious time and energy.

One major advantage you stand to gain when you take a stand is that you will be seen as being responsible. Everyone likes responsible people as they are easily trusted and can take charge of everything easily.

Take good care of yourself

Some of us find it very difficult to live a healthy life, which is one of the things people look at when they are trying to get to know you.

Apart from the fact that staying healthy is a vital aspect of getting people to like you, it is very important if you want to live longer and have a happy life. Staying healthy is not only good for your physical health but also good for your mental
ng.

I don't want to associate with an unhealthy person, and neither do you. Hence, these are the basic things we need to set in motion in trying to attract great friends.

Exercise

One of the easiest ways to keep fit and healthy is through regular exercise; the benefit of regular exercise cannot be overemphasized. There is a need for everyone, regardless of their gender, age grade, or physical strength to exercise in order to keep fit and look attractive.

A person who exercises regularly will feel better about their physical appearance, and this can help boost their confidence and self-esteem. When you go to the gym, for instance, you can form acquaintances with other gym members, and that might later develop into great friendship.

As a former personal trainer and current gym bunny who still takes pleasure in helping others to reach their exercise goals, you'll appreciate that I am a huge proponent of this. However, it might strike you as being a little vain. Surely people should like you for who you are, not what you look like, right? Yes, I'm all for that and I believe that we should not judge people on what they look like, but we're humans and we can't help doing it. It's human nature to judge on looks, and for the purposes of making a good impression it's important to look good.

Dress well

We discussed first impressions in the early part of this book. One of the criteria with which first impressions are judged is your clothes. The way you dress says a lot about you and can determine the caliber of people that are attracted to you if you attract them at all.

Hence, if are you on a quest to attract friends, be mindful of how you dress. It can determine if you will be successful in making friends or not.

There is a general notion that how you dress is how you are addressed. This means that if you want to be addressed in a respectable way, then your dressing should command respect.

Whatever occasion you are attending, dress for it.

Take note of what you are wearing before you step out of the house, and once you feel comfortable and confident in what you are wearing, then you can step out.

Practice personal hygiene

We have talked about this earlier, but I want to talk more about personal hygiene because it is so crucial when you want to make friends. This is one of the most important factors you should take care of in a bid to getting people to like you. Take care of yourself, practice personal hygiene, be clean, dress neat and decent. Spend time taking care of your hair and bath at least once daily.

We have talked about why you should dress properly in some sections above. In addition to proper dressing, keep yourself neat as well.

Besides the fact that good personal hygiene is pretty important to health, it does have a long way to go in your bid to make people like you. I am pretty sure you will not be comfortable talking to anyone with an unpleasant body odor. These are simple issues you should be mindful of and pay attention to in order to attract awesome friends.

Let's talk about some good personal hygiene habits.

Make it a habit to clean up every morning. Take a good thorough bath. You will feel good and confident about yourself before going about your daily activities. If you are a victim of body odor, have a good deodorant on. Keep in mind, how you present yourself (in terms of overall body hygiene) determines the kind of people you attract.

The gums and teeth are also susceptible to bacteria, so there is a need for us to always keep them clean by brushing them at least twice daily. To get better results and avoid tooth decay and gum disease, clean your teeth after breakfast and before retiring to bed. Do not forget to brush your tongue if you suffer from halitosis.

Try and maintain a low cut. But if you do want to keep your hair, make sure it is tidy. Invest in a good hair cream and hair shampoo. An unkempt hair is an invitation to dandruff.

Also, form the habit of washing your hands at intervals. This way, you limit your susceptibility to diseases and germs.

Make sure you wash your clothes with soap and water before wearing them again. One other easy way of getting rid of disease-causing bacteria is to dry your clothes in the sun. The sun will kill the germs.

The mouth and nose should be covered properly with a tissue while coughing or sneezing to avoid the spread of communicable germs in the air and food.

When you devote time and energy to taking care of yourself, you will attract great friends. You will give out the vibe that you are responsible enough to take care of yourself; hence, sustaining a relationship won't be an issue.

Once the aspect of your personal hygiene is well taken care of, then you should aim to exude positive energy whenever you are around people.

Exude positive energy

A positive thinker attracts good friends because they focus mostly on doing things that bring out the best in them.

Consistent positive thinking can actually reflect in your life, thereby becoming a part of you. This means that what you think about every day is what you turn out to be. So, if you are mindful of your day-to-day thoughts and avoid any kind of negative thoughts, people will want to be around you because they believe the positive energy will radiate into their life. After all, who wants to be around someone who is constantly complaining or saying bad things about others?

Believe in yourself and others. Practice positive thinking, and I am pretty sure you and your positive energy will attract amazing friends.

Be a Friend too

I know quite a lot of people who complain they don't have friends. When I talk with them, I discover that they are not so great at being a friend, let alone maintaining friendship. You can't expect a friendship to last if you don't make the effort to nurture it. Invest your time, your emotions, and yourself as well. Good and genuine friends are not easy to come by. Hence, you have to present yourself as a friend to attract and retain great friends.

It is not always easy to have a friend, especially a good one. You will have to take your time to develop a strong friendship because it deserves every bit of effort. To be a good friend, always be supportive of your friends and be true to your word. You will soon find that you are surrounded by positive and genuine people.

Join groups to meet people

Not just joining any group, but the right one, is a good step to take when trying to make friends. You will meet people with different views and interesting ideas that you can make friends with.

I talked about the gym in a section above. This is a terrific place to develop acquaintances that could lead to great friendships.

If you are a Christian, for instance, when you join a

group or subdivision in your local assembly, you may develop great friends.

Put yourself out there. Go and participate in different activities. You won't get to meet new and interesting friends if all you do is stay at home all day doing nothing.

Move past small talks

Don't get me wrong; I am not against small talk. But when it gets too lengthy, it becomes agonizing.

Move from small talks to deeper conversation. Be quick in asking someone you meet for the first-time deep questions so that you will be able to understand them fast.

You should also try to use deep questions to find out whether this is a person you really want to make friends with.

When you pass the conversational level of small talk, you are creating a bond that will leave a permanent impression on your counterpart. And if that happens, I am pretty sure the other person would love to have a conversation with you again.

In my book: *How to Talk to Anyone*, I teach people how to master small talks, how to move from small talks to "bigger" talks and develop long-lasting relationships. This is an important skill to develop because in the end, we want people not only to like us, but also to become our friends or even a long-term partner.

Display vulnerability

Showing vulnerability doesn't mean that you are weak; rather, it is a great way of getting acquainted with each other.

Opening up and disclosing the areas you are not too knowledgeable or comfortable talking is a good way to build a relationship.

Again, being vulnerable doesn't imply you are weak. It shows you have the courage to be who you are. Once people see your vulnerability, they will also open up to you and let you in on their secrets.

Value the time with the friends you have

Friendship, just like every other relationship, needs nurturing. You have to invest time and consciously make the effort to keep in touch. If you do not nurture it, you should not expect it to survive the test of time.

If you want to keep lasting and good friends you should try as much as possible to always be in contact with your friends frequently, no matter the distance. Thanks to technology, we can use social media to get in touch and schedule visits.

We should let our friends know that we value them. We don't need to be close to each other in order to value our relationship. A simple text message or call can always bring us together.

Connection leads to meeting new friends

Once you put all these tips into practice, I am pretty confident you will become a likeable person. If you are already a likeable person, with the tools and mindset I shared with you, people will enjoy your company even more.

Keeping in touch with old friends and connecting with them will provide the opportunity for meeting new friends. Keep in touch with your friends and always find time to hang out together.

Also, when you have the traits of a likeable person, you are likely to get invitations to places where you can meet other new people.

What We've Learned

- Everyone is unique. Be yourself and improve on your skillset; be very nice to people but don't over-please people. Set your standards.
- Stay fit and healthy because people are more attracted to those who take good care of themselves.
- To meet the right people, joining groups is a good idea. Always find the right group for the kinds of friends you want to make.
- To strengthen bonds, value the connections you have made and spend time with the friends you already have.

AFTERWORD

I am glad we made it to the end of the book. I hope by now you will be brimming with new confidence in your new skillset. I want to assure you that the techniques in this book are all techniques that I have counseled and taught many people for many years of practice.

I want to say a big thank you for coming with me this far on this journey! It's been an exciting and interesting experience for me, and I believe you also had a fun time learning all that was shared in this book.

When I was writing this book, I had you as a reader in mind and made the book as easy as possible so that both beginners and experts can benefit equally.

However, just reading the book won't be enough. You have to be practical to connect with other people. And like every other skillset, the more you practice, the more you will succeed. Therefore, I urge you to be open and willing to connect—then watch how your likability points change for the better.

The techniques are all proven to work, and there are many academic studies to back them; however, I have carefully selected the easiest methods that I have applied over the years.

I have taken the time to explain tested and proven tips that have worked for me and my friends. You have to understand the power of the first impression and make it work for you. People have less than a minute to decide if they like you or not. You also have to know how to employ simple nonverbal communication. It is a powerful tool in enhancing your relationships when meeting people.

People are naturally drawn towards similar persons; hence, this book has explained how to use this technique to make great friends. We have also discussed the importance of powerful small talk. You have to make the other party feel important by making the conversation about them. We have also discussed how to employ humor in lightening the mood when talking to people.

There is a section dedicated to being a friend yourself. This is the first and most important step in getting people to like you. You have to make efforts to work on yourself through personal hygiene and healthy lifestyle choices. When you are presentable and good-looking, people will be drawn to you. We have also dedicated a chapter to developing charisma. Developing charisma is more than being charming. It involves showing regard for people and being present during a conversation.

Remember not to tune out during a conversation, even if what the other person is saying is really boring and you desperately want to be elsewhere. Look at it this way: by giving this person your time you are showing, to others and yourself, that you can find the positives in anyone. That in itself is an attractive quality. So many people are quick to judge each other and focus on the negatives that it is refreshing when people come across a person who is genuinely positive and interested in everyone they meet. Persevere with that boring individual and you might find that they open up and reveal something deeper and a lot more interesting.

We have also examined the importance of self-confidence. This is reflected in many ways like the clothes we wear and our sense of purpose. In other words, you should have a goal and personal core values; this can be your driving force and personal principle that guides you every day. Developing your communication skills is also important. This involves guiding the conversation in the right direction and making others at ease with you.

Remember that making people like you is not fictional, magical, or an inborn gift. There are practical methods for you to become likeable after acquiring the skills necessary to engage people.

I believe that you have the potential to learn and master everything that is discussed in this book. Believe in yourself, commit to your daily practice, and you will attract many incredible friends who will stay with your for life.

AUTHOR'S NOTE

Thank you so much for taking the time to read my book. I hope you have enjoyed reading this book as much as I've enjoyed writing it. If you enjoyed this book, please consider leaving a review on Amazon. Your support really means a lot and keeps me going.

If you want more resources like this, follow me on my author profile on Amazon. You will find useful free tools for self development and success that will help you 10X your results.

ABOUT THE AUTHOR

Steven Hopkins is a personal trainer, entrepreneur, life coach, and author on a mission to awaken people to their innate talents and purpose so they can leave their mark in the world.

Steven holds a Master's degree in Behavioral Science and specializes in the areas of success, motivation, self-discipline, communication, NLP techniques, psychology, and human behavior.

When he isn't helping his clients attain their maximum potential, Steven Hopkins enjoys meditating, playing extreme sports, and traveling across the globe. He also loves spending quality time with his lovely wife and his two beautiful children.

Made in the USA
Columbia, SC
15 July 2019